PUFFIN BOOKS

UK I USA I Canada I Ireland I Australia
India I New Zealand I South Africa

Puffin Books is part of the Penguin Random House group of companies
whose addresses can be found at global.penguinrandomhouse.com.

www.penguin.co.uk
www.puffin.co.uk
www.ladybird.co.uk

First published by Puffin Books 2016
001

Written by Daniel Roy

Printed in Slovakia

A CIP catalogue record for this book is available from the British Library

ISBN: 978–0–141–36989–1

All correspondence to:
Puffin Books
Penguin Random House Children's
80 Strand, London WC2R 0RL

THE ULTIMATE
SURVIVAL
HANDBOOK

PUFFIN

INTRODUCTION

Welcome to Terraria, explorer! You can call me the Guide.

Guides like me have assisted millions of explorers, builders and adventurers over the years. You can always find me in the game if you want my advice, but if you're ever deep underground or lost in a strange land, just grab this book!

There are no quests or scores in Terraria. You decide what you want to do! You can explore distant biomes, travel the depths on the hunt for the Brain of Cthulhu, or build awe-inspiring structures to amaze your friends.

Because Terraria is such a vast, open world, it can be difficult to get your bearings at first. Don't worry! Follow this guide and we'll have you crafting Flamarangs and Phaseblades in no time.

CONTENTS

From time to time another ally will chime in with a specialized tip of their own. We're all here to help, after all. Yes, even the Angler!

CHAPTER ONE:
A WHOLE NEW WORLD

CREATING YOUR CHARACTER AND WORLD

Before you take your first step in Terraria, you have to create yourself and the entire world. No biggie!

SURVIVAL TIP

Always make sure you're in a safe spot before consulting the **Ultimate Survival Handbook**. You don't want a Zombie chewing on your arm while you're busy flipping pages, do you?

HOW HARD DO YOU WANT IT?

There are three different difficulty settings that affect your time in Terraria. You'll get to pick two during character and world creation, while the last one is tied to your game progress.

CHARACTER DIFFICULTY	EFFECT
Softcore	Drop half your money on death. (Can be picked up again.)
Mediumcore	Drop all your money and items on death. (Can be picked up again.)
Hardcore	Permanent death. No coming back!

Your character's difficulty setting determines what happens when you die. You can select it during character creation by clicking on the Softcore button.

WORLD DIFFICULTY	EFFECT
♥ Normal	Standard monster behaviour and health levels.
🗡 Expert	Monsters have twice the health and are more aggressive, but they also drop better rewards.

World difficulty determines how smart and deadly the monsters are. You can select it during world creation.

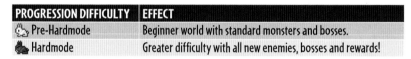

PROGRESSION DIFFICULTY	EFFECT
🐰 Pre-Hardmode	Beginner world with standard monsters and bosses.
🐾 Hardmode	Greater difficulty with all new enemies, bosses and rewards!

All worlds start in **pre-Hardmode** difficulty. To unlock Hardmode, you'll need to defeat the **Wall of Flesh** in the depths of the Underworld!

CREATING YOUR CHARACTER

There are hundreds of possible combinations when creating a new character in Terraria. You can use as many or as few of them as you want.

Click **Single Player**. Want to play the game with friends? No worries: characters you create in single player will be available in multiplayer too.

From the player selection menu, click **New**.

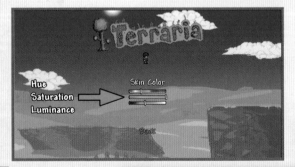

From the character creation screen, you can customize your **Hair**, **Eyes**, **Skin** and **Clothes** by clicking on each and adjusting the sliders. You can also switch between **Male** and **Female**. That little guy at the top is how your character currently looks.

STYLE TIP

Can't be bothered to create your own character, dear? Hit the Random option and you'll be good to go. If you're not happy with the results, hit Random again!

YOUR MUM GIVE YOU THAT HAIRCUT?

From the **Hair** menu, you can choose from fifty-one hair styles for your character. Click to cycle through them. Left-clicking moves forward, right-clicks go back.

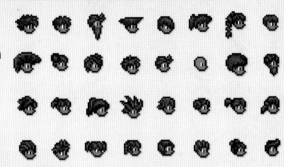

FIND YOUR STYLE

Under the **Clothes** menu is a button labelled **Style**. This allows you to change the types of clothes your character is wearing without changing the colours you've already chosen.

EVOLVE YOUR LOOK

You'll be able to change your appearance further as you progress through the game. Armour and Vanity items will all contribute to evolving your look over time.

You can also seek out a character called the Stylist who will let you dye your hair or choose one from a grand total of 123 funky hairdos. Look for her in Spider Nests.

ALL DONE!

Once you're happy with your character's basic look, it's time to wrap it up. Click Create, enter your character's name, then click on the little **Play** icon below your character portrait.

CREATING THE WORLD

Creating your own world in Terraria is pretty straightforward, since the game will take care of all the details for you. You have a few options to choose from, and then you'll be good to go.

From the **Select World** page, click on **New**.

IT'S A SMALL WORLD . . . MAYBE

Small (4200 x 1200 pixels)

Medium (6400 x 1800 pixels)

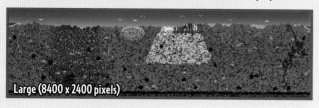
Large (8400 x 2400 pixels)

You can create a **Small**, **Medium**, or **Large** world.

Creating a large world has its advantages, especially for experienced players. Its varied environments offer more space to build and more riches to discover.

But small worlds have their own benefits too, and not just for new players. For one thing, a small world makes things easier to find. It also takes less of your computer's memory, which means it will load and save faster.

LET'S GET GENERATING

Once you've selected your difficulty level, it's time to name your world. Let your imagination run rampant, and then click **Create**.

Growing granite

Once your world has been generated, click on the **Play** icon below its name. Let's get you started on your grand Terraria adventure!

BEGINNER TIP

From the moment you enter the world, you'll have about eleven minutes of real-life time before night falls. If this is your first time playing the game, why not go over Chapter Two before you click Play, then build a shelter following the steps in Chapter Three?

CHAPTER TWO:
TAKE CONTROL

BASIC MOVEMENT AND CONTROLS

From jumping off cliffs to crafting magical swords, it's all at your fingertips.

CONTROLS OVERVIEW

The controls in Terraria are laid out so you can access them using your left hand, while your right hand is used to move and click the mouse.

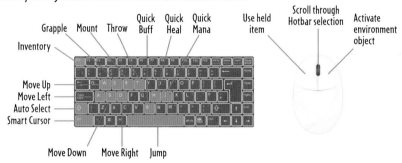

You can review these commands in-game too. To have a look, press **Escape**, click on **Settings**, then select **Controls**.

GETTING PLACES

Movement in Terraria is controlled using the **WASD** keys and the spacebar – you don't need the mouse to move around.

GO AHEAD AND JUMP. JUMP!

Press **Spacebar** to jump. To jump higher, hold the spacebar.

GOING DOWN?

To jump down from platforms, press **S**. This key is also used for climbing down ropes.

THE HOTBAR

The ten icons at the top left of the screen are your **Hotbar**. They allow you to switch between useful items without having to open the menu. Just tap the number corresponding to the item you want to select. You can also use your mouse's wheel to scroll through your Hotbar items.

NOT-SO-HOTBAR?

To change the items in your Hotbar, press **Escape**, then click on an item in your inventory. Click the spot you've chosen in the Hotbar to assign your new item to that position.

THE EQUIPMENT MENU

Your equipment is located to the right of the Inventory screen. From here, you'll be able to choose armour and items, and customize your looks. To use an item, simply drop it in the **Equipment** column.

If you've got yourself a piece of armour with great stats but are unhappy with the way it looks, simply place a better-looking piece of armour or Vanity clothing in the **Social** column. Items in these slots will not confer you any benefits, but you will appear to be wearing them.

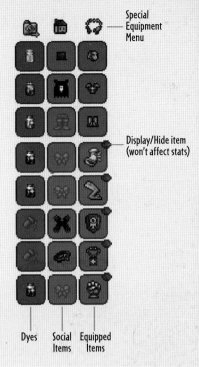

Special Equipment Menu

Display/Hide item (won't affect stats)

Dyes Social Items Equipped Items

STYLE TIP

Weary of helmet hair? Want to show off that glorious haircut I gave you? Craft Goggles or Sunglasses and equip them in your Social Helmet slot! You can also purchase a Familiar Wig from the Clothier for 1 Gold.

To customize your look even further, use **Dyes** to change the colours of your equipment. You can make Dyes using a **Dye Vat**, but for extra-special colours bring a **Strange Plant** to the Dye Trader.

SPECIAL EQUIPMENT

Clicking the **Special Equipment** button will bring up a section where you can select items with unique functions. These include pets that follow you around, light pets that provide illumination, faster Minecarts, rideable mounts and grappling hooks.

As with normal equipment, you can change the colours of your special equipment using **Dyes**.

Pet

Light Pet

Minecart

Mount

Hook

FUN TIP

There are tons of Vanity items to play with, ranging from animal costumes to seasonal attire for Christmas and Halloween. They're a great way to give your character a unique appearance.

INTERACTING WITH THE WORLD

You interact with every object in Terraria through your computer mouse. The rule is simple: you use the object you hold with the **left mouse button** and interact with objects in the environment by using the **right mouse button.**

Use held item

Activate environment object

To use an item in your inventory, simply click the corresponding number on the Hotbar, or press **Escape** to access the Inventory screen and click the item you want.

If you've selected anything besides a weapon, your cursor will turn into that item. Click where you want to use that item in the environment.

Clicking the left mouse button with a weapon equipped will use this weapon – often with bloody results.

Placing some torches

Wonder what's in that chest?

Objects in the environment can be activated by **right-clicking** on them. This includes talking to allies, opening doors and more. Your cursor will change to indicate an environment interaction.

BEGINNER TIP

You have to stand close to items to interact with them. If your cursor doesn't change when you place your mouse over an item, cosy up a little closer.

THESE ARE A FEW OF MY FAVOURITE THINGS

Worried about selling off your best Pickaxe by mistake? Hold the **Alt** key and click your favourite items in the inventory screen. The frame around the object means the item will not go into a chest if you click Quick Stack, won't be thrashed by mistake, and won't be thrown or deposited.

LET ME SELECT THAT FOR YOU

The **Left Shift** key is a godsend when mining resources. It will switch automatically between your Axe, Pick and Torches depending on what you're mining. It doesn't deselect your weapon either: no more scrambling for the Hotbar when a Slime makes a surprise appearance!

BEGINNER TIP

You don't need to hold down Shift after you start mining. Give that thumb or finger a rest . . . It deserves it.

CLICK SMARTER, NOT HARDER

Another way to automate mining and building is the **Control** key, which turns on **Smart Cursor**. When Smart Cursor is activated, your character will automatically select the appropriate spot based on your current tool.

SELECTED TOOL	EFFECT
Pickaxe	Mines a passage in the direction of your cursor
Axe	Chops the base of the tree or cactus nearest to the cursor
Hammer	Removes the wall nearest to the cursor
Block	Places a block nearest to the cursor
Wall	Places a wall nearest to the cursor
Platform	Extends an existing platform towards the cursor (creates staircase if cursor is diagonal)
Acorn	Plants an Acorn on a free spot
Minecart Track	Extends existing track
Wrench	Extends existing wire
Wire Cutter	Removes wire
Staff of Regrowth	Plants grass or moss nearest to the cursor

Mining downward with Smart Cursor

COMBAT

Combat in Terraria is as easy as selecting a weapon and clicking your mouse. You'll be doing a lot of clicking, so get that finger ready.

UP CLOSE . . .

To swing a melee weapon such as a sword, make sure it's selected on your Hotbar and click anywhere on the screen. You will swing your weapon and hopefully hit something.

. . . AND FAR AWAY

You can shoot a ranged weapon by selecting it on your Hotbar, then clicking in the direction you want to shoot. Want to shoot a Zombie in the face? Just click at it.

LOADING UP

You can select the type of ammo you'll fire off by opening the Inventory menu. Place the ammo types from top to bottom in the order you want to use them. Once you run out of one type of ammo, you'll automatically switch to the next one.

CRAFTING

Crafting in Terraria is a complex subject that deserves its own chapter. Heck, I could write a whole book about it! Hmm, there's an idea . . .

For now, let's check out the basic controls for crafting any item. Bring up the Inventory page by pressing **Escape**.

Crafting Menu

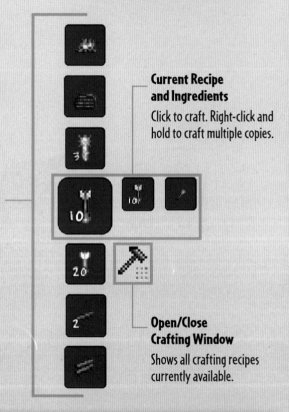

Current Recipe and Ingredients

Click to craft. Right-click and hold to craft multiple copies.

Available Recipes

Click to select for crafting.

Open/Close Crafting Window

Shows all crafting recipes currently available.

CRAFTING TIP

Can't see an item you'd like to craft? Either you're missing recipe components or you need to move closer to the required crafting station.

CHAPTER THREE: THE FIRST DAY

SURVIVING YOUR FIRST DAY IN TERRARIA

Welcome to Terraria! Beautiful place, isn't it? You've got about eleven minutes before the Zombies attack.

From the moment you enter your world, the clock is ticking. You have approximately eleven minutes to gather resources and build a shelter. When night falls, Zombies and Demon Eyes will spawn and try to kill you, unless you're somewhere safe.

BEGINNER TIP

Don't worry too much if you don't manage to build a shelter in time. If you do die, you'll just respawn near me (unless you're playing in Hardcore mode).

STEP ONE: GET CHOPPING

You can use any material you want to build a shelter, but **Wood** is the easiest to get right now. Select your **Axe** in the Hotbar and click on the bottom square of a nearby tree. Hold your mouse button until the tree disappears – excellent chopping! – and then gather the fallen wood.

Luckily, trees are readily available in most worlds. Keep hacking until you have about **150 Wood**. This should be enough to build your shelter and associated items, as well as improve some of your arsenal.

STEP TWO: MAKE A WORK BENCH

I'm about to send you on the hunt for Slimes, and unfortunately that **Copper Shortsword** isn't quite going to cut it. Let's craft you a better one out of those trees you just chopped. Press Escape to access the Crafting menu and create a **Work Bench**.

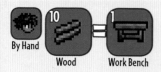

By Hand | Wood 10 | = | Work Bench 1

To craft items with the Work Bench, start by placing it in your Hotbar, select it, then place it on the ground. If Autopause is not enabled in your Options menu, you can just open the Inventory, click the Work Bench, and click on the ground to place it.

Now let's get you a better sword!

Congratulations, you just crafted your first item in Terraria!

STEP THREE: WE'RE GONNA NEED A BIGGER SWORD

When you stand next to the Work Bench or any other crafting station, you'll have access to many new recipes. One of them is the **Wooden Sword**, which is a major upgrade from your basic Copper Shortsword.

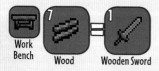

Work Bench | Wood 7 | = | Wooden Sword 1

As you see in the recipe, crafting this sword requires the Work Bench. Make sure you're standing close enough to it, then go to your Crafting Menu.

STEP FOUR: SLIME TIME

To finish your shelter, you're going to need one more ingredient: **Gel**. With it you'll craft a Torch, which you'll use to light up your shelter.

Do you see those green or blue blobs bouncing around? Odds are you've already had to dispatch one. Those are **Slimes**, and they drop the Gel you need. If you don't see one nearby, walk around and you should see one in no time.

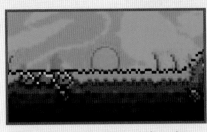

A Green Slime, plotting your slimy doom

Select your **Wooden Sword** from your Hotbar and then approach a Slime. Wait for it to pounce and right-click your mouse to take a swing. Repeat until the Slime is dead. You should now have automatically picked up some Gel!

SURVIVAL TIP

You can't swing your sword while moving, so be sure to stand still when you're close enough to the Slime. Additionally, you'll need to click repeatedly to take multiple swings.

STEP FIVE: LAY THE FOUNDATIONS

Now that you have plenty of Wood and one Gel, you've got all you need to start building.

Select your **Pickaxe** and start flattening an area at least twenty squares wide, digging one block below ground level.

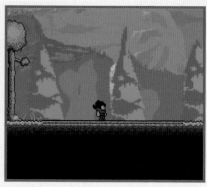

Once that's done, select **Wood** from your Hotbar and build a simple rectangular structure:

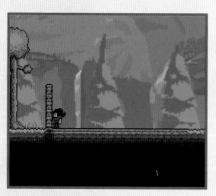
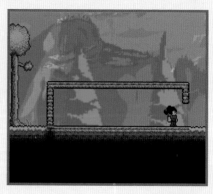

Leave enough space for your character to walk out, as shown in the last picture. That's where you'll put the door.

BEGINNER TIP

To pick up the Work Bench or any other placed item, select your Pickaxe and use it on the item. This will put the item in your inventory. Weird, huh? Just think of the Pickaxe as the tool you use to pick up resources from the environment.

STEP SIX: IS IT DRAFTY IN HERE?

For the next step, we're going to craft a few other things.

In order for a dwelling to be considered a House your allies can live in, you'll need an entrance, a flat surface, something to sit on, and some light.

Go back to your **Work Bench** and craft a **Wooden Door**, a **Wooden Chair** and about **60 Wood Walls**.

Oh, and pick up that **Work Bench**, too. You're going to want to bring it inside the shelter.

Now, go back to your shelter, and place the **Work Bench** there. Next, place the **Wooden Door** in the entrance. Remember: to place an object, first place it in your Hotbar, then select it.

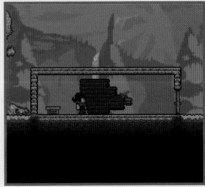

Next, use the **Wood Wall** to build the back wall.

BEGINNER TIP

Smart Cursor makes this task super easy. Turn on Smart

You now have a shelter that will protect you against Zombies and other monsters (providing you keep the door closed, that is). But now we're going to make it into a home.

Craft a **Torch** and place it anywhere in the House.

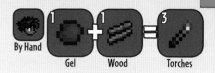

By Hand | Gel | + | Wood | = | Torches

Congratulations! You're now the proud owner of a House!

Once night falls, feel free to point and laugh at the Zombies knocking at your door. Go ahead, you deserve it!

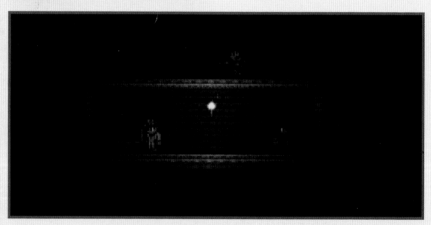

Sorry, there's no Mr Braaaaaaaains at this address!

VETERAN TIP

Houses in Terraria serve to attract and retain useful allies. See **Chapter Six: Building** for more details.

CHAPTER FOUR: EXPLORATION

THE GREAT OUTDOORS

There's a big, exciting and dangerous world out there. Let's go check it out!

GENERAL ADVICE

EXPLORE BY DAY . . .

The daytime is best for exploring the surface. Make sure to check out the many caverns, as they contain Chests and precious treasure. Two super useful items to look out for are the **Hermes Boots**, which will allow you to sprint, and the **Cloud in a Bottle**, an item that lets you double-jump. Another great item is a **Magic Mirror** or an **Ice Mirror**, as both allow you to teleport back to your spawning place whenever you want.

But **Magic Mirror** or none, just make sure to be safely home by sundown – unless you're itching to take part in a Zombie scuffle!

. . . DIG BY NIGHT

Although some pesky monsters may follow you into the tunnels, the narrow passageways make it much easier to ward them off.

EXPLORATION GEAR

GOT A LIGHT?

When digging underground, always make sure to bring a big quantity of Torches to light your way. Chop down trees for **Wood**, and hunt Slimes for **Gels**.

VETERAN TIP

Light Pets are special pets that follow you around and provide illumination. **Shadow Orbs** and **Crimson Hearts** sometimes drop one when you destroy them, or you can buy a **Magic Lantern** from the **Skeleton Merchant** at night on a full moon.

PLATFORMS: NOT JUST FOR SHOES ANY MORE

Wooden Platforms allow you to build bridges across chasms and reach otherwise unreachable spots. Be sure to stock up on these on the surface as wood is rare underground.

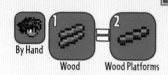

By Hand — Wood — Wood Platforms

FOR THAT HEALING TOUCH

It's a good idea to bring healing items with you. You'll eventually discover or craft your own potions, but in the meantime, look around the surface and gather some **Mushrooms**.

BEGINNER TIP

You don't want to rid the world of trees, do you? Replant some of those **Acorns** you get from chopping trees, and healthy replacements will pop up in no time.

HANGING FROM A THREAD

You'll find **Rope** in Chests and Pots around the world, as well as from Slimes. Always keep a stack of Ropes on you, as they help you move vertically until you get a grappling hook.

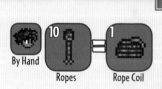

By Hand — 10 Ropes — 1 Rope Coil

With 10 Ropes, you can craft a **Rope Coil**, which allows you to place Rope more quickly. Select it and click on a block to anchor ten segments of Rope to it.

USING THE MAP

Lost? Looking for something? Check the map!

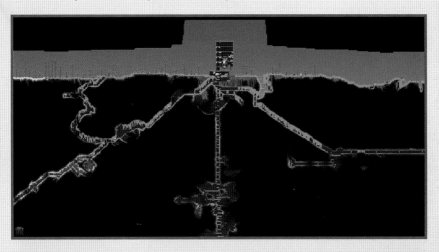

M — Open map

PgUp PgDn — Adjust minimap transparency

- + / - = — Zoom in/out

⇥ — Cycle through minimap styles (Portrait, Overlay, Off)

W A S D — Move around (when map is open)

WORLD OVERVIEW

The world of Terraria is made up of various environments called **biomes**, arranged on top of one another in **layers**. Together, all these biomes make for the tasty layer cake we call the world.

SPACE

The upmost layer, with nothing much in it except, you know . . . space.

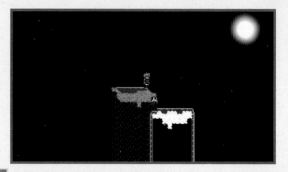

SURFACE

The surface is where you'll find most biomes in Terraria. These include Forest, Snow, Desert and Jungle, as well as either one of the evil biomes: Corruption and Crimson.

UNDERGROUND

The Underground is the area just beneath the surface. The surface's biomes extend into the Underground, meaning that if you dig below the Desert, for example, you'll find a Desert-like underground.

CAVERN

The cavern layer is the vastest in Terraria. Enemies you encounter here get harder to beat the deeper you go. You'll also hit lava on the lowest levels – which is a little like water . . . but worse.

UNDERWORLD

Welcome to Hell . . . literally. The bottom layer in Terraria is also a biome in its own right. It's a dangerous place filled with lava and nasty demons, in addition to precious Hellstone.

SURFACE BIOMES OF TERRARIA

Terraria is a diverse place. Let's take a look at some of the biomes you'll encounter on your expeditions throughout the universe . . .

FOREST

Most newcomers to Terraria start out in the Forest biome. It's a tranquil place during the day, with only a few Slimes to make your life difficult.

COMMON MONSTERS

Green Slime

Blue Slime

Purple Slime

Zombie

Demon Eye

UNCOMMON MONSTERS

Pinky

Goblin Scout

COMMON RESOURCES

Wood

Mushroom

SNOW

It's possible you started the game in the Snow biome instead of the Forest. Things are pretty much the same here, except chillier. Even the Zombies dress for the weather around these parts!

COMMON MONSTERS

Ice Slime   Zombie Eskimo   Demon Eye

COMMON RESOURCES

Boreal Wood   Silverthorn

DESERT

The barren Desert is a trickier biome than Forest or Snow. The Desert features **Cactus** instead of Wood, which you can use to create better (and cooler-looking) armour and weapons.

COMMON MONSTERS

Vulture   Antlion   Sand Slime

Antlion Swarmer   Antlion Charger

COMMON RESOURCES

Cactus   Waterleaf

JUNGLE

The Jungle is one of the hardest environments you'll find on the surface, so it's better to stay clear until you've upgraded your equipment a little. For the same reason, be careful when digging down to the Underground Jungle, as the monsters here are much tougher.

COMMON RESOURCES

Rich
Mahogany

Moonglow

COMMON MONSTERS

| Jungle Bat | Piranha | Jungle Slime | Snatcher | Zombie | Demon Eye |

OCEAN

If you make it all the way across the map you'll reach the Ocean biome, marking the left and right limits of your world. There are some good rewards to be found at the bottom, but make sure to come up for air . . . and watch out for **Sharks**!

COMMON RESOURCES

Palm Wood

Coral

COMMON MONSTERS

| Shark | Jellyfish | Crab | Sea Snail | Squid |

EVIL BIOMES

These biomes are bad news! They are a part of your world that has become twisted by evil. Monsters here are much tougher, so you should proceed with caution. Early in the game, it's better to turn the other way when you run in to an evil biome.

THE CORRUPTION

Not only are the monsters in the Corruption bad news, but the biome also features deep, dangerous chasms. Once you've significantly improved your equipment you'll want to explore the bottoms of those chasms, as they contain **Shadow Orbs**, which you can destroy to summon the Eater of Worlds, as well as **Demon Altars** to craft boss-summoning items.

COMMON MONSTERS			COMMON RESOURCES		
Eater of Souls	Devourer	Corrupt Goldfish	Ebonwood	Vile Mushroom	Deathweed

CRAFTING TIP

One way to breathe underwater is to craft a **Gills Potion**. You'll need **Coral** from the Ocean floor and **Waterleaf** from the Desert. Acquire Bottled Water by opening the Crafting menu near open water, then use a **Bottle** to craft the potion.

THE CRIMSON

The red-hued cousin of the Corruption, the Crimson, also features twisting caves and mean flying monsters. Proceed with extreme caution. The bottoms of these caves contain **Crimson Hearts** which you can destroy to summon the Brain of Cthulhu, as well as **Crimson Altars**, which you can use to create boss-summoning items.

COMMON MONSTERS

Crimera

Face Monster

Blood Crawler

Blood Feeder

COMMON RESOURCES

Shadewood

Vicious Mushroom

Deathweed

YOUR FIRST UNDERGROUND EXPEDITION

Caves and caverns contain many useful objects that will help you as you progress through the game. Exploring nearby caverns should be your first priority. Can't find one? Dig your own hole. Either way, make sure to bring plenty of **Torches**, **Wooden Platforms**, **Mushrooms** and **Rope**!

A promising-looking cave entrance

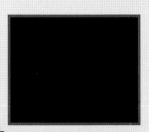

LIGHT THE WAY
Getting too dark? Place a Torch. No point in working in the dark and risking falling down an unseen shaft!

MINE YOUR OWN BUSINESS
You're looking for ores such as Copper, Tin, Iron and Lead. If you spot a deposit, it's worth going out of your way to mine them.

BEGINNER TIP

Auto Select makes it easy to place Torches. Hold **Left Shift** and move your cursor to an empty space. You will automatically hold a Torch, which you can then click to place.

ALWAYS HAVE AN EXIT STRATEGY

Use Blocks or Wood Platforms to build staircases across chasms or holes, or swing a Rope to climb back up a vertical shaft. You wouldn't want to be caught without a way back to the surface!

Digging upward to escape the water

DEADLY WHEN WET

One of the underground hazards facing the brave miner is water. If you fall into water, don't panic! It takes a while to drown. Just climb out of the water using Rope, Blocks or Wooden Platforms, or dig upward at an angle to escape the water. Just be sure to get your head out of the water before your air bubbles all fade away!

DIG YOUR OWN HOLE

You don't have to strictly follow the caves and caverns, either. Use your Pickaxe to dig your own tunnels. Make sure you save the blocks you mine for crafting and building!

CRYSTAL HEARTS

Spread throughout the world are **Crystal Hearts**. Breaking one will yield a **Life Crystal**, which you can use to get an extra 20 Life. Not only will this increase the odds of your survival, but once you use your first Life Crystal, the Nurse will move in to one of your available Houses.

BEGINNER TIP

Smart Cursor and **Auto Select** are amazingly useful when digging. Activate Smart Cursor by pressing **Left Control**, then hold **Left Shift** to Auto Select the Pick. Let go of the Shift key, and keep the mouse pointer in the direction you want to dig.

THE DUNGEON

Venture far enough either left or right above the surface, and you'll encounter the entrance to the **Dungeon**, an underground labyrinth filled with unique monsters and treasure. To enter the Dungeon, you'll need to talk to the Old Man at night and defeat **Skeletron**, one of the biggest, baddest bosses in the game.

VETERAN TIP

As much as I'd like you to lift my curse, I don't recommend fighting Skeletron unless you have at least 300 Health and 10 Defense. You'll just get yourself killed, stranger.

MINI-BIOMES

Here are some of the interesting sights you'll encounter as you explore the world above and below. These environments, called mini-biomes, offer unique monsters and rewards.

SPIDER NEST

Spider Nests are small underground areas covered with Cobwebs and nasty spiders. This is where you'll encounter the **Stylist**, who went exploring without her scissors and got herself in a tight spot. Just talk to her to free her.

STYLE TIP

If you free me from the spiders, I'll thank you by moving into an available House. You'll be able to buy Dyes from me, as well as access all-new hairstyles!

BEEHIVE

Beehives can be found in the Jungle Underground. Destroying the **Larva** inside will summon **Queen Bee**, a powerful boss with some great rewards. Careful where you swing that sword until you're ready to face her, though! The Larva can sometimes hide at the bottom of a pool of Honey.

Hitting this little guy will make his mum very cross.

/ING TREE

gigantic trees hide unique treasure deep down in their roots.
, take a look!

ENCHANTED SWORD SHRINE

These shrines usually contain a fake sword, but one time out of three you'll find a powerful sword called the **Enchanted Sword**. If you're really lucky, you might even get **Arkhalis**, a legendary sword that deals continuous high damage in the direction of your cursor when you hold the mouse button.

FLOATING ISLAND

You can reach these high-perched cloud islands using a **Gravitation Potion** or by building a long bridge high up in the sky extending in either direction. You'll find **Skyware Chests** on some of these islands, which contain useful items such as the **Shiny Red Balloon** or the **Lucky Horseshoe**.

MUSHROOM CAVE

These glowing underground caves contain **Glowing Mushroom**, an essential ingredient in crafting **Healing Potions**.

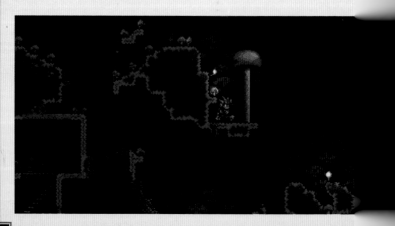

CHAPTER FIVE:
CRAFTING

CREATING YOUR OWN ITEMS

See all those resources you've been gathering? It's time to put them to good use!

CRAFTING ESSENTIALS

As you explore Terraria, you'll gather resources that can be turned into useful items like armour, weapons and potions.

NEED A RECIPE? ASK THE EXPERT

Found a curious object? Keen to know what you can craft with it? Ask me! Simply right-click on your Guide, select **Crafting**, and drag the item in the empty window in the Crafting area. I'll give you a list of ingredients and the crafting station you need.

MAN YOUR STATIONS

Except for a few things such as Torches and Wood Platforms that you can craft by hand, you'll need various **crafting stations** for creating most items. You can craft the majority of stations yourself, but some - such as the Demon Altar or the Hellforge - can only be found. I'll get to those in a moment ...

BASIC STATIONS

Work Bench

Furnace

Anvil

Sawmill

Loom

Cooking Pot

COMBINATIONS

Chair and Table

Chair and Work Bench

Bottle and Table

SPECIALIZED CRAFTS

Keg

Heavy Work Bench

LIQUIDS

Water

Lava

Honey

NON-CRAFTABLE STATIONS

Demon Altar

Crimson Altar

Alchemy Table

Imbuing Station

Tinkerer's Workshop

Hellforge

Dye Vat

THEMED FURNITURE CRAFTING

Bone Welder

Glass Kiln

Honey Dispenser

Ice Machine

Living Loom

Sky Mill

Solidifier

CRAFTING YOUR STATIONS

You'll need a full suite of crafting stations to progress in Terraria. Here's how to create the essential ones.

WORKHORSE: THE WORK BENCH

If you built your shelter, then you're already familiar with the Work Bench. It's one of the most useful crafting stations in the game.

By Hand

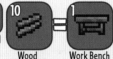
Wood — Work Bench

STYLE TIP

Tired of the boring old Work Bench? You can craft it using a variety of woods such as Boreal, Palm and Rich Mahogany. Look in the Dungeon for unique, non-craftable Work Benches!

SPIN THE BOTTLE: THE BOTTLE CRAFTING STATION

To brew potions, place a Bottle (or Vase, Mug or Cup) on furniture with a flat surface such as a Table or Dresser.

CRAFTING TIP

Want to save space in your crafting room? Here's a Goblin trick: place your Bottle on the Work Bench!

STAND THE HEAT: THE FURNACE

A Furnace enables you to smelt ores into bars and craft Glass from Sand. It even doubles as a light source.

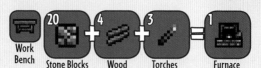

Work Bench • 20 Stone Blocks + 4 Wood + 3 Torches = 1 Furnace

TEMPERED STEEL: THE ANVIL

The Anvil is where you'll put those metal bars to good use. This is the crafting station you'll use to create better weapons, armour and tools.

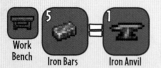

Work Bench • 5 Iron Bars = 1 Iron Anvil

Work Bench • 5 Lead Bars = 1 Lead Anvil

TERRARIA TRIVIA

You can craft an Anvil from either Iron or Lead, depending on which ore your world features. Besides their names and colours, the two work exactly the same.

SAWDUST EVERYWHERE: THE SAWMILL

The **Sawmill** allows you to craft cool furniture beyond the basic tables and chairs that the **Work Bench** provides.

Anvil • 10 Wood + 2 Iron/Lead Bars + 1 Chain = 1 Sawmill

OTHER CRAFTING STATIONS

SOFT AS SILK: THE LOOM

The Loom lets you create Silk from Cobwebs, as well as many cool-looking clothes.

 Sawmill

 12 Wood

 = 1 Loom

TIME FOR TEA: THE COOKING POT

This pot allows the creation of food items that will grant you a Buff called **Well Fed**, which boosts your combat abilities.

 Anvil

 10 Iron/Lead Bars + 2 Wood

 = 1 Cooking Pot

COLOUR YOUR WORLD: THE DYE VAT

The Dye Vat allows you to create Dyes and Paints that change the colours of objects. You can purchase it from the **Dye Trader**. See **Chapter Seven: Allies** for details.

CHAIR COMBINATIONS

You can use a **Chair** along with a **Table** or **Work Bench** to craft **Watches**, **Goggles** and **Sunglasses**. Watches tell the time – while Goggles and Sunglasses are mostly for appearance.

STYLE TIP
Wear Sunglasses out in the sun for a cute little surprise!

EVIL CRAFTING: DEMON AND CRIMSON ALTARS

Demon Altars and **Crimson Altars** allow the crafting of boss-summoning items such as the **Suspicious Looking Eye**. Your world will feature only one type, depending on whether you have the Corruption or the Crimson. Look for them underground, especially in evil biomes.

COMBINATIONS GALORE: THE TINKERER'S WORKSHOP

The Tinkerer's Workshop lets you meld the abilities of different objects into powerful new combinations. You can purchase it from the Goblin Tinkerer. See **Chapter Seven: Allies** for details.

FROM HELL: THE HELLFORGE

The Hellforge works exactly like your basic Furnace, except it also lets you smelt **Hellstone**. You can pick your own Hellforge down in the buildings of the Underworld.

UPGRADING YOUR GEAR

Each type of metal has a corresponding set of swords, armour, bows and tools that you can craft with them. As soon as you have enough Bars, you should craft better weapons and armour, then create an improved Pickaxe. Better Hammers and Axes are nice, but do them last of all: they are not as critical as the rest.

Weapons, armour and tools made out of different metals get increasingly more powerful the rarer the metal. Metal is organized in tiers: the higher the tier, the more powerful the equipment you can make with it.

TIER	MATERIAL		WHERE TO FIND THEM
1	Copper	Tin	Surface Underground Cavern
2	Iron	Lead	Surface Underground Cavern
3	Silver	Tungsten	Underground Cavern Floating Islands
4	Gold	Platinum	Underground Cavern Floating Islands
5	Demonite	Crimtane	Underground Cavern Eye of Cthulhu Eater of Worlds (Demonite) Brain of Cthulhu (Crimtane)
6	Meteorite		From meteorite crash site
7	Hellstone		Underworld

MINING ADVANCED ORES

Upgrading your Pickaxe is crucial because it speeds up your mining. Additionally, some of the rarer ores can only be mined with the better Pickaxes. To mine **Demonite Ore** or **Crimtane Ore**, for example, you'll need either a **Gold** or **Platinum Pickaxe**.

PICKAXE TYPE	CAN MINE . . .							
	Common Ores	Meteorite	Demonite/ Crimtane	Hellstone/ Obsidian	Ebonstone/ Crimstone	Dungeon/ Bricks	Desert/ Fossils	Cobalt/ Palladium *
Copper	X							
Tin	X							
Cactus	X							
Iron	X							
Lead	X							
Silver	X							
Bone	X	X						
Tungsten	X	X						
Gold	X	X	X					
Platinum	X	X	X					
Nightmare	X	X	X	X	X	X	X	
Death-bringer	X	X	X	X	X	X	X	
Molten	X	X	X	X	X	X	X	X
Reaver Shark	X	X	X	X	X	X	X	X

* Cobalt Ore and Palladium Ore are only available in Hardmode.

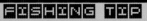

FISHING TIP

Notice something . . . fishy with the **Reaver Shark**? If you want it, you'll have to fish it out of the Ocean yourself. Just try not to get eaten by one of its cousins!

OTHER COOL CRAFTING RECIPES

Here are some useful tools to build as you progress through the game.

HOOKED ON A FEELING: THE GRAPPLING HOOK

Press 'E' to fire your Hook at the cursor. Jump to disengage it.

This super-useful tool will let you scale walls with ease. You can craft Grappling Hooks with more range using gems, but this basic Grappling Hook gets the job done.

Anvil — Hook 1 + Chains 3 = Grappling Hook 1

The **Hook** drops from Skeletons, Undead Miners, Piranhas, Hoplites and Undead Vikings. As for the **Chain**, you can craft it at an Anvil using 1 Lead or Iron Bar.

TIME IS ON MY SIDE: WATCHES

No more missing your bedtime! **Watches** will tell you the time of day as long as you have them in your inventory. This Copper Watch isn't very precise, but it'll get you started; use more advanced metals to craft better watches.

Chair + Table — Copper Bars 10 + Chain 1 = Copper Watch 1

GOING FOR A SWIM: DIVING GEAR

This item may just save your life on an underwater cave-exploring expedition. With the Diving Gear equipped, you can jump repeatedly to swim up to the surface from even the deepest pools. It also greatly extends your air supply.

Tinkerer's Workshop — Flipper 1 + Diving Helmet 1 = Diving Gear 1

You'll find the **Flipper** in Chests, especially Water Chests. As for the **Diving Helmet**, there's always a chance one of those Sharks swallowed one by mistake . . .

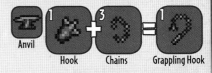

SURVIVAL TIP

A **Gills Potion** will make your search for the Flipper and Diving Helmet much easier. You can craft it from **Coral** from the Ocean and **Waterleaf** from the Desert. Be sure to keep an eye on that potion timer!

CHAPTER SIX: BUILDING

CONSTRUCTION IN TERRARIA

From massive castles to gravity-defying works of art, the only limit in Terraria is your imagination! Well . . . that and construction materials.

CONSTRUCTION TIPS

A SLIPPERY SLOPE
Use a **Hammer** to create bricks with a slope. Hit the same brick repeatedly to go through all available angles.

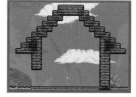

TEAR DOWN THIS WALL
The Hammer is also used to remove background walls. Simply select your Hammer and click on the background to remove it.

> ### CONSTRUCTION TIP
> The **Smart Cursor** really speeds up breaking down walls. Tap the **Left Control** key and hold down the mouse button.

THERE GOES GRAVITY
New blocks can only be placed next to existing blocks. There is an easy way to create 'floating' platforms, though! Just build a support first, then remove it with your Pickaxe.

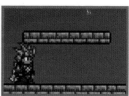

FAST TRANSIT

Minecart Tracks are just the thing if you want to get from A to B in a hurry. Once they're placed, you can use Minecart Tracks by right-clicking on them, then use the **Left** and **Right** keys to move.

Anvil   Iron/Lead Bar   Wood   Minecart Tracks

Use your Hammer on the end of the track to change it. The **closed** track end will stop your cart, while the **bumper** end will bump you right back in the opposite direction. As for **open** tracks, be careful: ride through one and your Minecart will fly right off the rails!

Minecart Track ends: closed, bumper and open

You can create intersections for your tracks, allowing you to create complex track networks. When going through an intersection, hold the **Up** or **Down** buttons to choose which branch to follow.

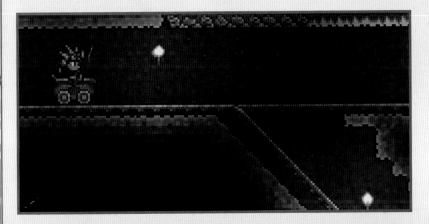

CRAFTING TIP

If Minecart Tracks are still too slow for you, you can craft a **Minecart** using 15 Iron or Lead Bars and 10 Wood. You can then put it in your Minecart slot in your Special Equipment. The Mechanic also sells **Booster Tracks**.

BEDROOM CONSTRUCTION

Now that you've got the outside sorted out, let's look at interiors!

Bedrooms are special constructions that let you set your spawn point where you want. When you re-enter the world or when you die, you'll return to your Bed instead of the starting point.

MAKE YOUR BED

The central component of a bedroom is, of course, the Bed. You can craft a Bed using all sorts of Wood. You can even make one out of Mushroom, Meteorite or Marble! You'll need a Loom to make the Silk first.

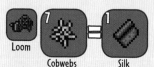

Loom   Cobwebs **7** = Silk **1**

Sawmill   Wood **15** + Silk **5** = Bed **1**

GO TO YOUR ROOM!

To function as a bedroom, a room must have a proper background wall and enough space for you to appear at the foot of the bed. You also need an entrance such as Wooden Platforms or a Door.

Once your bedroom is ready, place the bed and right-click on it. If the room is usable, you'll get the message **'Spawn point set!'** You're good to go!

A basic bedroom

CONSTRUCTION TIP

You can't use a natural background wall (such as sand or a cave wall) to create a bedroom; it has to be an artificial wall that you place yourself. Cosy.

BEGINNER TIP

It's a good idea to always leave at least one suitable House unoccupied. This way, new allies will be able to move in automatically as they become available.

HOUSING YOUR ALLIES

Allies need a House to live in. While preparing for your first night in Chapter Three, I had you build a simple structure suitable for a Guide like me, but there are a lot of other options for housing us.

WHAT MAKES A HOUSE
In order for a structure to qualify as an ally's House, it needs to fulfil a few simple conditions:

1. It's made up of at least sixty tiles (including the exterior walls)
2. It has a background wall
3. It has a Light Source, a flat surface and a Chair
4. It's not too close to the Corruption or the Crimson
5. It's closed off to the outside, either with blocks or Wooden Platforms

A simple House

MINIMUM SIZES
All these building shapes will be sufficient to qualify as a house. The number of tiles in each structure includes the exterior walls.

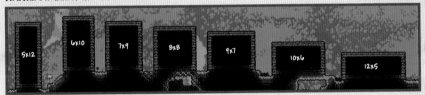

USING THE HOUSING QUERY
At the top right of your Inventory screen is the Housing Tool. Click on the **question mark** to select the Housing Query, then click on a structure. This will let you check if the structure qualifies as a House.

SETTING AN ALLY'S HOME
In the Housing menu, click on an ally's face to select it, then click on the House you want to assign to them. You'll see who lives in which House by their portrait on the wall. If you want to kick an ally out, just right-click on their portrait.

Ahhh ... Home sweet home.

HOME DECORATION

BUILDING WITH STYLE

With nearly 200 different blocks to craft or mine, there's no limit to what you can build in Terraria. Want to live in a vampire's castle? How about a treehouse? Don't throw away the blocks you mine, put them to good use!

PAINT THE TOWN RED

You can personalize your constructions further by using **Paint** and **Wallpaper**. Speak to the Painter: he has all the colours and tools you need.

FURNITURE WITH A THEME

Want a Cactus Chair? How about a table made of Honey or Slime? While you can craft most pieces of furniture using the Sawmill, some require special crafting stations.

STATION	NAME	THEME	HOW TO GET IT
	Bone Welder	Bones	Check the Dungeon's Chests
	Glass Kiln	Glass	Craft it using the Anvil
	Honey Dispenser	Honey	Look for Ivy Chests in the Underground Jungle
	Ice Machine	Frozen	Investigate Frozen Chests
	Living Loom	Living Wood	Check the roots of gigantic Living Trees
	Sky Mill	Sky	Explore Floating Islands for Chests
	Solidifier	Slime	Fight King Slime for it

ADVANCED CONSTRUCTION TOOLS

If you want to get serious about building, here are a few tools of the trade that will make life easier. The Traveling Merchant doesn't always have all items in stock; check out his inventory whenever he comes by.

INCREASE YOUR RANGE

Three items will allow you to place blocks further from yourself: the **Toolbelt**, the **Extendo Grip** and the **Toolbox**. You can use all three together too. You can get the Toolbelt from the Goblin Tinkerer and the Extendo Grip from the Traveling Merchant, but to get the Toolbox you'll have to wait for Christmas season, as it can only be found by opening Presents.

SPEED THINGS UP

The **Brick Layer** will speed up the placement of blocks, while the **Portable Cement Mixer** will make placing background walls a breeze. The Traveling Merchant sometimes sells these items, so check his inventory often!

Another way to speed up construction work is by using a **Builder Potion**. It will extend your range a little bit too.

CRAFTING TIP

Using the Tinkerer's Workshop, you can combine the **Brick Layer**, **Extendo Grip**, **Paint Sprayer** and **Portable Cement Mixer** into the **Architect Gizmo Pack**, which combines the functions of all four.

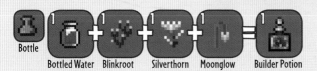

Bottle — Bottled Water + Blinkroot + Silverthorn + Moonglow = Builder Potion

TAKE YOUR MEASURE

The **Mechanical Ruler** will lay a grid on your screen to help you line things up. The Mechanic sells it.

For the **Ruler**, check with the Goblin Tinkerer. You can use it to measure distances.

CONSTRUCTION TIP

From Christmas decorations to subway systems, Terraria players worldwide certainly have a lot of brilliant ideas! Visit Terraria's official website at **www.terraria.org** for more building inspiration.

DOWN THE WIRE

Once you rescue the Mechanic from the Dungeon, you will have access to powerful new building tools. By using a **Wrench** and some **Wires**, you can wire objects and trigger them or turn them on and off using **Pressure Plates**, **Levers** and **Switches**.

Objects that can be wired and triggered include **Lanterns**, some **Statues**, **Active Stone Blocks**, and even walls when using **Actuators**. Building possibilities using wiring tools are near-infinite: some crafty players have even created computer logic systems!

BASE DEFENCE
Architectural beauty isn't everything, though. When the going gets tough, you want a base that will withstand the most formidable army with ease. Here are a few ideas to defend your home turf.

SHUT THAT DOOR!
Unless the Blood Moon is out or the Goblin Army is on the march, monsters won't be able to open doors. Wooden Platforms are useful as ceilings, but they make it easy for the Zombies to sneak in, so be careful where you place them.

STAY INDOORS
The main reason for placing background walls is that monsters won't appear indoors. Make sure every room in your base has a full background wall.

GET OFF THE GROUND
Take advantage of the floating block trick to build your base up in the sky. Ground enemies won't be able to reach your base this way. Just make sure you can get back in!

So long, Zombies!

IT'S A TRAP!
By now you've probably encountered those annoying **Dart Traps** that shoot you full of poisoned darts. Use them to your advantage! Wire them up with a Lever – or better yet, connect them to a timed trigger. Just make sure to stay out of the way when you turn it on!

CHAPTER SEVEN: ALLIES

THE HELPFUL PEOPLE OF TERRARIA

Trouble in Terraria? Your friends are here to help.

You have many friends out in the world who want to offer advice or sell you great items at a discount. Not all of us are as easy to find as yours truly, though. In this chapter, I'll let your allies tell you where to find all of us.

BEGINNER TIP

We allies are sometimes referred to as **NPCs**, which stands for 'Non-Player Characters'. It's a bit like calling your friends 'non-me people', though, isn't it? Personally, I prefer the term 'allies'.

ALLY CHECKLIST

FOUND?	ALLY		NICKNAME	SERVICES
✔			The Guide	Provides helpful tips and crafting instructions
			The Merchant	Sells a variety of goods
			The Nurse	Heals you on request
			The Demolitionist	Sells explosives
			The Dye Trader	Sells Dyes and dyeing equipment
			The Dryad	Provides items related to nature, Corruption and Crimson
			The Arms Dealer	Sells Guns and Bullets
			The Stylist	Allows you to change your hair colour and style
			The Painter	Sells Paints, Wallpapers and painting tools
			The Angler	Offers fishing quests and rewards
			The Goblin Tinkerer	Sells the Tinkerer's Workshop, reforges items
			The Witch Doctor	Sells the Imbuing Station and the Blowgun
			The Clothier	Sells clothes
			The Mechanic	Supplies wiring tools
			The Party Girl	Sells party items

TERRARIA TRIVIA

Notice I'm not there? You'll need to make it to Hardmode to find me!

MEET THE NEIGHBOURS

Without further ado, let's introduce ourselves!

They say there's a person who will tell you how to survive in this land . . . Oh wait. That's me

THE GUIDE

Howdy! I'm the first ally you encounter in the game, and I'm here to guide you through even the most difficult spots.

WHERE TO FIND ME
You can find me wandering around your spawn point at the beginning of the game. I'll move right in with you once you build your first shelter.

MY SERVICES
You can always come to me if you're stuck and need some advice. You can also show me an item and I'll tell you what you can craft with it, free of charge.

TERRARIA GOSSIP

Something strange is going on with the Guide . . . The Nurse told me she had to treat him for lava burns a few nights ago, yet no one saw him leave his House. It sounds like the work of an evil magic . . . I bet you could find the answer in the Underworld!

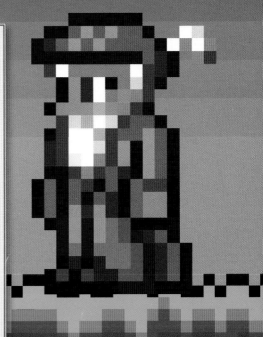

You want apples? You want carrots? You want pineapples? We got torches.

THE MERCHANT

Need a Torch or a Lesser Healing Potion in a hurry? Come see me! I sell a variety of goods, both common and exotic. I can also buy some of your unused items and sell them overseas for a (small) profit.

WHERE TO FIND ME
I'll move into an empty House as soon as you have 50 Silver to your name. I gotta make a living, you know!

MY SERVICES
I sell a wide variety of wares ranging from potions to **Piggy Banks** and **Bug Nets**. I also have the basic Copper tools in stock if you ever lose yours.

BEGINNER TIP

The Merchant sells the **Mining Helmet**, which features a useful headlamp. At 4 Gold it's a bit expensive, but definitely worth the investment.

THE NURSE

When you fall of a cliff and need a fix-up, I'm your gal! Just come by when you're injured and I'll patch you right up for a small sum. Hey, a girl's gotta eat!

WHERE TO FIND ME
You'll need to show some dedication to your health before I arrive. Find a **Crystal Heart** to raise your Life to 120 and then we'll talk.

MY SERVICES
Besides sewing limbs back on and saving you from the brink of death, I'll also remove any affliction that's tormenting you.

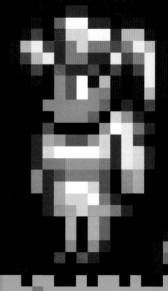

You look half digested. Have you been chasing Slimes again?

THE DEMOLITIONIST

When it comes to explosions, the bigger the better! I've got everything you need right here to blow half the world's monsters sky high!

WHERE TO FIND ME
I can smell gunpowder a mile away. As soon as you have an explosive such as Dynamite, a Bomb or a Grenade in your inventory, I'll move right next door. Hope you don't mind the noise!

MY SERVICES
I mostly sell Grenades, Bombs and Dynamite. My stock is the bomb!

Check out my goods; they have explosive prices!

THE DYE TRADER

Looking to enliven your tired attire with a dash of colour? Come see me and I'll show you the world's most vibrant hues and tones!

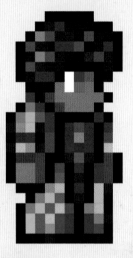

I bring you the richest colours in exchange for your riches!

WHERE TO FIND ME

I don't move around for undiscerning clients, you know. You'll need to find a **Strange Plant** or defeat a major boss for me to show up. I also require that you carry some manner of dyeing ingredient before I move in.

MY SERVICES

My wares include the **Dye Vat**, as well as a variety of cheerful and appealing colours. If you bring me **Strange Plants**, I'll even share my most exotic and exclusive Dyes.

THE DRYAD

The Corruption and the Crimson must be stopped at all costs! I'm here to assist you in your journey to purify this world once and for all.

WHERE TO FIND ME
I'll join your cause once I know you have what it takes. Defeat **Eye of Cthulhu**, **Eater of Worlds**, **Brain of Cthulhu** or **Skeletron** and I'll move in.

MY SERVICES
I sell a number of nature items including seeds and nature-themed walls. I also sell **Purification Powder**, which you can use to turn an evil block back to its natural state.

I'm also useful when you come under attack near my home. I'll bestow my **Dryad's Blessing** upon you, raising your Defense and damaging enemies.

What's this about me having more 'bark' than bite?

VETERAN TIP
The Dryad can also tell you how hallowed or evil your world is. This becomes especially relevant once you enter Hardmode.

THE ARMS DEALER

Hey there, buddy. I got all the Guns and ammo you need right here. This stuff is nothing like the stuff the Demolitionist is selling; I'm all about long-range precision.

This ain't a movie, pal. Ammo is extra.

WHERE TO FIND ME
I'll show up to sell you Bullets once you've got something to fire them with. This means any Gun that uses Bullets as ammunition.

BEGINNER TIP

Probably the easiest way to get a Gun is to smash **Shadow Orbs** in the Corruption or **Crimson Hearts** in the Crimson. These have a chance to drop the Musket or the Undertaker respectively.

For you I think we'll do something . . . low maintenance.

THE STYLIST

Hey there, pet. If you want to do something with that tangled web you call hair, just drop by my place and I'll freshen you up!

WHERE TO FIND ME
I'm always getting myself in trouble, so you'll most likely find me stuck in a **Spider Nest** somewhere. Free me and I'll move right next door. We can gossip together!

Looks like I got myself in a sticky situation . . .

MY SERVICES
Come by any time you want to update that haircut, hon. I have over 123 styles to choose from, as well as a variety of hip hair Dyes that'll do wonders for your hair.

THE PAINTER

Add a splash of colour to your life! With my tools and supplies you'll be able to paint blocks, background walls and even furniture whatever colour you want.

No, no, no . . . There are TONS of different greys! Don't get me started.

WHERE TO FIND ME
I'll move in as soon as you have eight other allies living in your Houses. I need lots of customers to support my painting business!

MY SERVICES
I sell all the essential painting tools: the **Paintbrush**, the **Paint Roller** and the **Paint Scraper**. I also have Paint in all the colours of the rainbow, some nice-looking Wallpapers and some art pieces to liven up your world.

THE ANGLER

Hey there, fish bait! Looking to make a quick buck? Then grab your fishing pole, cos I got just the thing for you!

WHERE TO FIND ME
I like to take naps near the Ocean or floating around on the soothing waves. Something about the sound of the surf makes me slee– Zzzzz.

I don't have a mummy or a daddy . . . but I have a lot of fish! It's close enough.

MY SERVICES
Er, you're still here? Anyway, ask not what the Angler can do for you, ask what you can do for the Angler! I have tons of ideas for dangerous, I mean, *fun* quests you can do for me every day. I'll even throw in some money and rewards if you entertain me enough!

FISHING TIP

All you need to fish is a **Fishing Pole** and some **Bait**. To catch bait, grab the **Bug Net** from the Merchant and look around for bugs and critters. Spot an open body of water and cast your line!

THE GOBLIN TINKERER

Hello, friend! I bring to you the wonders of Goblin technology! I'm a master Goblin engineer and I can help you combine your existing items in exciting new ways.

WHERE TO FIND ME
You'll find me in the tunnels of the Cavern layer after you've defeated a Goblin Invasion. (See **Chapter Eight: Monsters** for details.) I've had, ah, a falling out with my fellow Goblins, and they've abandoned me in the tunnels below the surface.

Yo, I heard you like rockets and running boots, so I put some rockets in your running boots.

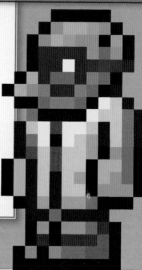

I only told them they weren't going east . . .

MY SERVICES
I sell some interesting items including the **Tinkerer's Workshop**, which allows you to combine items in unexpected ways. You can also ask me to reforge your items: this will change the bonus on your equipment, hopefully to something more useful.

TERRARIA TRIVIA
Notice something familiar about the Clothier? He bears a striking resemblance to the Old Man at the entrance of the Dungeon. Guess we know what happens to him once he is freed from his curse!

> The heart of magic is nature. The nature of hearts is magic.

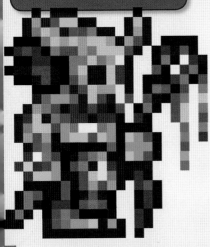

THE WITCH DOCTOR

Interested in the Jungle's dark powers, are you? You've come to the right place . . .

WHERE TO FIND ME
I'll join you once you prove your mastery over the forces of nature. Defeat **Queen Bee** and I will join your cause.

MY SERVICES
With my **Imbuing Station**, you can craft Flasks that improve the power of your weapons. You can also shoot Seeds and Poison Darts using my deadly **Blowgun**.

THE CLOTHIER

I used to live a troubled life, but no more! Now all I care about is fabrics, cuts and exquisite attire. If you want to dress up, come by for a fitting.

WHERE TO FIND ME
You'll have to defeat **Skeletron** at the entrance of the Dungeon before I show up in a vacant House. Good luck!

MY SERVICES
I sell only Vanity items: clothes of all kinds as well as Threads to craft your own. My fineries won't help you in a fight, but you'll look great as you bleed all over the place.

> Life is like a box of clothes. You never know what you are gonna wear!

THE MECHANIC

Hiya! I've got everything you need to wire up your creations. From Pressure Plates to Wire Cutters, I'm your one-stop shop for a wired world.

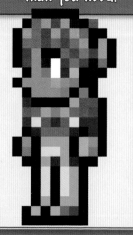

> Always buy more wire than you need!

WHERE TO FIND ME
I'm a curious gal who gets in all sorts of trouble. Look for me in the Dungeon. Take your time . . . I've almost got Wi-Fi going down there.

MY SERVICES
I've got everything you need for wiring, from **Wires** to triggers, **Wrenches** and **Actuators**.

> I can't decide what I like more: parties, or after-parties.

THE PARTY GIRL

Enough crafting and building, let's paaaarty! I've got all the party tricks and favours you need, from Bubble Machines to Fireworks Boxes. Woohoo!

WHERE TO FIND ME
I like to be fashionably late to the party. I'll show up once all the other allies described in this section show up. Then it's party time!

Yeeeeah! That's more like it!

MY SERVICES
I've got Confetti Guns! I've got Bubble Machines! I've got Beach Balls and Fireworks! Let's get this party started!

TERRARIA TRIVIA

The Party Girl is the final ally you can acquire before Hardmode. Once she's moved in, you know you've found everyone!

WANDERING ALLIES

These two allies will help you on your journey, but unlike the rest of us, they won't stick around and move in.

I don't refund for 'buyer's remorse'. Or for any other reason, really.

THE TRAVELING MERCHANT

The Traveling Merchant shows up randomly at dawn with useful and rare items that change every visit. The Traveling Merchant will start showing up once you have at least four allies living with you. Make sure to check out his wares every time he comes by – you never know what you might find!

You would not believe some of the things people throw at me . . . Wanna buy some of it?

THE SKELETON MERCHANT

The Skeleton Merchant shows up from time to time in underground tunnels. He provides useful exploration items such as **Lesser Healing Potions**, **Torches**, **Bombs** and **Rope**. He also sells rare items such as yoyo **Counterweights** and the **Magic Lantern**, depending on the time of day and the phase of the moon.

CHAPTER EIGHT

MONSTERS

TERRARIA'S BOSSES AND HOW TO DEFEAT THEM

Ready to kick some butt? Here's how!

CRAFT BETTER WEAPONS AND ARMOUR

Always make sure you have the best possible armour set and weapon available. These should take priority over tools such as the Axe or even the Pickaxe.

RAISE YOUR LIFE

Throughout the world are **Crystal Hearts**. Break them with your Pickaxe to get a **Life Crystal**. Use it to raise your Life by twenty points. You can bring your Life up to 400 using this method.

RAISE YOUR MANA

Mana is what powers magical weapons such as staffs, so having more of it will give you that much more firepower. You can raise your Mana easily to 200 by crafting **Mana Crystals**. Just gather **Fallen Stars** at night: they fall all over the world's surface.

By Hand   Fallen Stars   Mana Crystal

REFORGE YOUR EQUIPMENT

Once you acquire the **Goblin Tinkerer**, you can talk to him to reforge your weapons and equipment, making your attacks faster and deadlier, or your Defense higher.

STOCK UP ON POTIONS

Always come to battle with a full stock of Healing and Mana Potions. If you find **Glowing Mushrooms**, you can use them to upgrade your **Lesser Healing Potions** to **Healing Potions**, and similarly with **Lesser Mana Potions**.

Other potions can boost the stats you need for a particular fight. For instance, when fighting Brain of Cthulhu or Skeletron, a **Swiftness Potion** can help you dodge incoming attacks.

You can also use the **Cooking Pot** to prepare fish like Bass, Trout and Salmon into items that will give you a bonus in battle.

KING SLIME

The king of all Slimes is thirty times the size of a regular Slime. He's one of the easiest bosses you'll fight in the game, but he's fun to fight and a great way to gather tons of Gels in a hurry.

SUMMON HIM

You'll sometimes encounter King Slime in the outer edges of the map, or if you kill enough of his minions on days when Slimes rain from the sky.

A certain way to summon him, though, is to craft a **Slime Crown**.

BEAT HIM

Just like any other Slime, King Slime likes to jump around a lot. Treat him like a ten-tonne Slime and you should be fine. Watch out for the Blue Slimes he ejects as you hack into him, though, as they can easily overwhelm you. Also, be careful not to get too far away from King Slime: if he can't reach you, he'll teleport right on top of you instead.

His Slimy Highness

LOOT HIM

King Slime drops some Slime-related items like the useful **Slime Hook** and the **Solidifier**, as well as a great mount, the **Slimy Saddle**. He also drops **Ninja Armor**!

TERRARIA TRIVIA

Why ninja gear? If you look closely at King Slime, you'll notice a ninja caught inside. Wonder what happened to the poor guy . . .

EYE OF CTHULHU

Here's an eye tooth that has nothing to do with dentistry. Make sure you have **Silver** or **Tungsten Armor** or better before facing this boss, and equip a long-range weapon with plenty of ammo. If you've found **Jester's Arrows**, all the better.

SUMMON HIM

If you have more than 200 Life and 10 Defense, there's a chance the Eye of Cthulhu will come looking for you at night. If you just can't wait for this joyous occasion, gather **Lenses** from his buddies the **Demon Eyes**, then use the **Suspicious Looking Eye** at night.

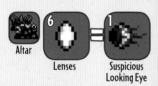

Altar · 6 Lenses · = · 1 Suspicious Looking Eye

TERRARIA TRIVIA
Before you ask: it's pronounced 'kuh-THOOL-hoo.'
Try not to bite your tongue while saying it!

BEAT HIM

When the battle begins, the Eye of Cthulhu will stay back for the most part, sending miniature version of himself called **Servants of Cthulhu** after your blood. Once he falls below half his health, though, he'll turn into a chomping terror and try and take a bite out of you.

In both cases, mobility is key. Start the battle on an open plain, and fire at him from a distance as you dodge his attacks.

Eye of Cthulhu's toothy second form

LOOT HIM

The Eye of Cthulhu will most likely be your first reliable source of **Demonite** or **Crimtane Ore**, allowing you to craft powerful new weapons like Light's Bane or the Tendon Bow. But to craft other Demonite or Crimtane items, you'll first need to defeat the Eater of Worlds or the Brain of Cthulhu for other materials.

EATER OF WORLDS

The Eater of Worlds is a giant worm that lurks at the heart of the Corruption. He's a pretty tough fight, but you'll need to defeat him if you want to craft better weapons, armour and tools using the **Demonite Ore** he drops.

SUMMON HIM

The easiest way to summon the Eater of Worlds for the first time is to shatter three **Shadow Orbs** at the bottom of the shafts in the Corruption. Since you won't have a powerful enough Pickaxe at this point, you'll need to use **Bombs** to reach them. You can also purchase **Purification Powder** from the Dryad and use it on Ebonstone Blocks to turn them to regular Stone.

DEMOLITION TIP

Throwing Bombs around is fun and everything, but if you need precision destruction, combine **Bombs** and **Gels** to make **Sticky Bombs**.

BEAT HIM

You'll need to destroy each of the Eater of World's fifty segments in order to beat him. If you destroy a middle segment, the Eater of Worlds will split into two smaller worms: for this reason, it's better to concentrate on the head or the tail.

Weapons that strike multiple targets such as the **Vilethorn** or **Jester's Arrows** are especially useful here.

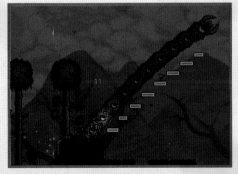

Sneak attack!

LOOT HIM

The Eater of Worlds drops a steady supply of **Demonite Ore** and **Shadow Scales**, allowing you to craft all Demonite items including Shadow Armor and the Nightmare Pickaxe.

BRAIN OF CTHULHU

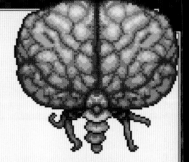

If the Eye wasn't enough, this brainy monstrosity is sure to give you a splitting headache. He's the Crimson equivalent of the Eater of Worlds. You'll need to face him to progress as he drops precious **Tissue Samples** and **Crimtane Ore**.

SUMMON HIM

The easiest way to summon the Brain of Cthulhu is to shatter three **Crimson Hearts** down in the pits of the Crimson. You'll need **Bombs** to blast through Crimstone unless you have a **Deathbringer Pickaxe** or better. You can also use **Purification Powder**, purchased from the Dryad, to turn Crimsand into regular Sand.

BEAT HIM

You'll need to move around a lot to survive this one. When the fight starts, the Brain himself is invulnerable, leaving you to deal with an army of **Creepers**. Take them out while avoiding the Brain's teleport attack to reach stage two.

Big Brainer is watching you.

Brain of Cthulhu: 317/1000

The Brain of Cthulhu opens its mind's eye

In the second phase, the Brain opens up and is now vulnerable. Hit him with all you've got while dodging his attacks to claim your prize.

LOOT HIM

With the **Crimtane Ore** and **Tissue Samples** the Brain drops, you'll be able to craft all Crimtane items including Crimson Armor and the Deathbringer Pickaxe.

QUEEN BEE

The Queen Bee is a pretty tough boss that you can summon inside Bee Hives in the Underground Jungle. Defeat her and you'll be rewarded with some sweet, unique bee-themed items.

SUMMON HER

Once you find a Bee Hive in the Underground Jungle, keep an eye out for a **Larva**. Destroy this to seriously irritate its mum. Can't find the Larva? It sometimes hides in pools of Honey. Jump in there and swing a sword until the Queen Bee appears.

BEAT HER

The Queen Bee has two modes of attack: she'll either fly at you in a straight line, fly around and sting you, or hover in place and bombard you with stingers. Objects that help you move faster or jump higher, such as **Hermes Boots** or a **Cloud in a Bottle**, will help dodge her attacks. You can also stand in Honey pools around the hive to help regenerate your health.

LOOT HER

The Queen Bee drops a great number of powerful bee-themed items including the **Bee Gun**, a bow named **The Bee's Knees** and the **Bee Keeper Sword**. She also drops **Bee Wax**, which you can use to craft the **Bee Armor**.

SKELETRON

Skeletron is the guardian of the Dungeon and the toughest boss in the pre-Hardmode world. Killing him will grant you access to the Dungeon and free the Old Man from his curse. You should have top armour and weapons, as well as 400 Life, before you tackle this boss.

SUMMON HIM

To fight Skeletron for the first time, you'll need to have a chat with the Old Man at night.

VETERAN TIP

Don't even think about entering the Dungeon without first beating Skeletron. The Dungeon's guardian would kill you instantly!

BEAT HIM

Skeletron is made of three parts: his head and his two hands. You only need to destroy the head to beat him, but taking out the hands makes that easier. Make sure to dodge his attacks, especially when the head is spinning – in that phase his Defense is low, but his attacks are deadly.

This boss is quite an armful.

LOOT HIM

The main interest in beating Skeletron is accessing the Dungeon. However, from time to time he'll drop a grappling hook called **Skeletron Hand**, as well as a magic weapon, **Book of Skulls**.

EVENTS

Once you start raising your Life and taking out Shadow Orbs or Crimson Hearts, the world will present you with new dangers and opportunities.

THE GOBLIN ARMY

Once you smash your first **Crimson Heart** or **Shadow Orb** and have at least 200 Life, there's a chance the goblins will come marching on your base. You'll have to defeat eighty of them to defeat the invasion. Defeating the Goblin Army the first time will unlock the **Goblin Tinkerer**.

THE BLOOD MOON

You know you're in for a bad night when the moon turns red and it starts raining blood. The Blood Moon will remind you of the night terrors of your early days as the Zombies finally figure out how to use a doorknob. Blood Moons start to happen once you raise your Life to 120 or more.

METEOR STRIKE

Once you destroy your first **Shadow Orb** or **Crimson Heart**, there's a chance a meteorite will crash-land on your world. This is a great opportunity to acquire precious **Meteorite Ore**. Beware, though: Meteorite Ore burns until it's mined, so either mine it carefully from a distance or use fire protection such as an **Obsidian Skin Potion** or an **Obsidian Skull**.

Watch out for the **Meteor Heads**, also. They don't take kindly to intruders . . .

WHAT'S THAT YOU GOT THERE, FRIEND?

That Guide Voodoo Doll . . . It looks exactly like me! You say one of those Voodoo Demons in the Underworld had it? How is that possible?

Whatever you do, please don't drop it in lava! Who knows what would happen if you did! And not just to me . . . Something terrible could rise from the depths of the Underworld! And were you to defeat it, things would never be the same again . . . **Congratulations, you've made it almost all the way to Hardmode! Once you defeat the Wall of Flesh, your world will enter Hardmode, offering all-new monsters, allies, crafting material and treasure.**

Check out these websites for extra help, building inspiration and more!

OFFICIAL WEBSITE
www.terraria.org

FACEBOOK PAGE
www.facebook.com/TerrariaOfficial

TWITTER ACCOUNT
www.twitter.com/Terraria_Logic

COMMUNITY FORUMS
forums.terraria.org

OFFICIAL TERRARIA WIKI
terraria.gamepedia.com

TERRARIA ON REDDIT*
www.reddit.com/r/Terraria

TERRARIA WIKIA*
terraria.wikia.com

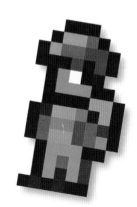

* Websites not monitored by Re-Logic. Enter at your own risk!